DOCUMENTING
BUSINESS and PERSONAL INFORMATION
of
SMALL BUSINESS OWNERS

An Offline Ready-Reference

Teresa M. O'Brien

Printed in the United States of America.
ISBN: 978-0-9791577-8-3
First printing, 2021.

O'Brien Consulting Group, LLC
Midland, MI

Table of Contents

INTRODUCTION

I first started collecting some of this information when I started my own company in 2004. I have continued to add and update the information over time. I have no family living within 100 miles of me so if anything were to happen, my siblings needed to know what information to look for and where to find the details. So, I started a version of what I am now giving you in this book, including where to find all the supporting information (summary and detail) both in my house and at a safety deposit box. I included key contact information for my solo operation consulting business in my summary.

I became especially committed to keeping this updated after my mother had a stroke in December 2006. I realized how quickly things can change in a person's life and others could need to immediately step in and help. It was important to know what medicines my mother was taking, any medical conditions that she had, etc. Electronic medical records are often incomplete or wrong. Plus many times information doesn't transfer accurately from one medical care facility to another, even when the information is being transferred at the same time as the patient.

Since my brother and I had been helping our Mom for years with her finances, we both knew where things were. Not everyone has that luxury when a crisis requires them to step in and help. I also saw how important it was to have her medical information at my fingertips. My sister, who is a nurse and was my Mom's POA, was able to talk with medical staff and get her the right care.

I became even more motivated to collect all this information after 2010 when my mother died and I was responsible for settling her estate. It is not to be expected that my siblings would know where I bank, who my business colleagues are, or details of my medical situations. The document in this book is a way for me to summarize the most important information. I periodically send them each an updated copy for their files so they have it at their own homes and don't have to travel to my house before they can start working on my situation. This will allow them to focus on helping me with a minimum of disruption in their lives.

They have had a key to my house for decades. This way they can quickly gain access to any details that they need while having a summary document to work from until they arrive. As the baby boomer generation moved away from our homes in search of jobs, we are separated from many of our siblings. This means that I am not the only person who is distanced geographically from family members who would likely be the ones to step in and help in an emergency.

HOW TO USE THIS BOOK

The book has three main sections: business resource information, personal financial, and medical. The first part of this workbook is business-related. The business section allows for information about customers, vendors, and employees. The medical section gives you an opportunity to summarize your key medical information: allergies, medicines, surgeries, underlying health conditions, and the latest lab work results.

The tables are a way to document your information for whoever is to help you in a crisis. We all know things about our best friends and close family members, but we may either not know everything that is needed or we don't have all the relevant details right at our fingertips. You get to decide how much you want to share.

CAUTION: Because this information can be used for identity theft, please keep it safely locked up when you are not working on it.

Note: The book is separated into business, medical, and other personal information. Because the information in the book is separated, you can give each area to different people to handle the separate areas.

READ THIS FIRST
LOCATION OF KEY DOCUMENTS

This section should include two types of information: an overall approach to where to find information (medical and money) and location of key information needed immediately for a person to get started (phone and computer passwords, medical, purse/wallet, password list). This might also include the name of your landlord. This is likely to be the information that they will be standing in your house frantically looking to find. It will also make it easier for you to do quick updates. Useful personal information to list here are date of birth, social security number, any previous names, medical insurance cards location.

Date Last Updated:

ITEM	KEY INFORMATION
Original documents	
Keys	
Computer password	
Phone password	
Password location	
Home safe	
Medical	
Purse/Wallet	
Monthly statements	
Check registries	
Last year's tax papers	
Electronic Equipment	

BUSINESS INFORMATION

KEY BUSINESS CONTACTS AND CLIENTS

This can include key clients if you are a solo entrepreneur, as well as any committees or boards that you sit on. If you aren't a solo business owner, then you can list contact information for the head of each department and/or your business partner(s).

NAME	COMPANY	SERVICE	PHONE	EMAIL

KEY VENDORS

List any companies whose services you routinely use. Include your accountant, lawyer, advisors, insurance rep, web designer, publicity, retail stores, utilities, phone and internet service, and any other key vendors. Also include banks and brokerages where you have business lines of credit or accounts, 401k accounts, business insurance, etc.

INSTITUTION	ACCOUNT NUMBER	TYPE OF ACCOUNT	FILE LOCATION	CONTACT INFORMATION

OTHER KEY BUSINESS INFORMATION

Include some basic information such as the name of the company, type of business, business location, keys, leases, main phone number, websites, and social media accounts for the business. Also, include access to voicemail and email. Other information that might be included here is PO Box, storage units, disposition of your business, any co-owners of the business, location of business tax records, and financial records from the most recent year. Also, include any previous business that you are no longer a part of and any (if any) ongoing responsibility for liabilities of that company.

This is a good place to note any clients who owe you money. Also, identify those who take care of updating your books and doing your taxes, or any paperwork that you are required to file (when and to whom), and the location of articles of incorporation. It would also be good to note the names of any board members, properties owned by the business, your company tax ID number, the landlord for your business location, and mortgage holder on any mortgages or business loans that your company has.

ITEM	LOCATION	COMMENTS

ITEM	LOCATION	COMMENTS

PERSONAL INFORMATION

KEY PERSONAL CONTACT INFORMATION

List your key friends, family members, and neighbors in this table. Include the ones that you are in frequent contact with. They can then let others in that group know any information. Include home, cell, and work numbers for ease of contact. Include not only their contact information but also how they can help.

KEY FRIENDS & NEIGHBORS	HOW THEY CAN HELP	CONTACT INFORMATION

MOST OFTEN NEEDED DOCUMENTS

List the location of the paperwork for each of these items, if they are relevant to your situation. There will be opportunities later in this book to articulate contact information for some of these items.

ITEM	LOCATION
Will	
Trust	
Social Security card	
Bank statements (recent)	
Investment account statements (recent)	
List of Users names & passwords	
Credit card list	
Car insurance	
Post Office box agreement & key	
Adoption papers	
Divorce agreement/decree	
Naturalization papers	
Marriage license	
Military discharge papers	
Passport or citizenship papers	
Birth certificates of minor children	
Life insurance policy numbers	
Rental property leases	

Safe-deposit box number and key	
Deeds	
Storage locker contract and key	
Loan statements (recent)	
Annuity contract numbers	
Tax returns (last 2 years)	
Motor vehicle titles	
Employee benefits information	
Military service records	
Mortgage statements (recent)	
Homeowner's insurance	
Record of assets	
Health insurance	
Business ownership/interest documents	
Prenuptial agreement	
Car lease agreement	
Postnuptial agreement	
Naturalization papers	
Voter registration card	
Airline mileage numbers	
Personal papers from 4-17 years ago	

INCOME

List all your personal sources of income. This includes the money that you receive from your business (owner's draw), NOT the amount of money that your company makes.

You can adapt this to your situation – consulting, retail, or manufacturing. If you are a solo business practitioner, you might want to provide more detail here by customer. If you have a company with multiple employees who can help fill in details when needed, then an average income from your company will suffice. You should also include any money that is owed to you and is being repaid periodically (rent from income-producing property or money from repaying a land contract).

TYPE	SOURCE	CONTACT INFORMATION	CURRENT AMOUNT	HOW PAID
Owner's Draw				
Pension				
Social Security				
Veteran Admin				
Alimony				
Stocks, Bonds, Mutual Funds				
Annuity				
401K				
403B				
Traditional IRA				

TYPE	SOURCE	CONTACT INFORMATION	CURRENT AMOUNT	HOW PAID
Roth IRA				
SEP				
SIMPLE				
Rental				
Royalty Fees				

EXPENSES

List all of your personal expenses. This includes medical, utilities, credit cards, charge cards, debit cards, mortgages, loans, taxes, insurance, etc. It is good to identify whether an actual check needs to be written or whether it is autopay and from which account.

INSTITUTION	SERVICE/ PRODUCT	ACCOUNT NUMBER	PAYMENT TERMS	PAPERWORK LOCATION	CONTACT INFORMATION

INSTITUTION	SERVICE PRODUCT	ACCOUNT NUMBER	PAYMENT TERMS	PAPERWORK LOCATION	CONTACT INFORMATION

INSURANCE

There are so many types of insurance that a person can have and some of those might be able to be used in a crisis (health, auto, life, homeowners, long-term care, cancer, and miscellaneous). For example, your long-term care policy might include a provision for a stay at a rehab facility. So list each type of insurance that you have and the key contact information. The emergency situation will then determine which can and should be used.

It is good to note which medical insurance is primary and which is secondary if you have more than one.

COMPANY	POLICY NUMBER	PAYMENT TERMS	CONTACT INFO	INFORMATION LOCATION

LEGAL INFORMATION AND DOCUMENTS

Include the location of the will, trusts, living will/advanced directive, patient advocate, and power of attorney. Also include contact information for your lawyer. Include information on prepaid funeral expenses.

DOCUMENT	COMMENTS

FINANCIAL ASSETS

These are the resources that you can use beyond your income and insurance to pay for whatever services you need. You want to include checking accounts, savings accounts, CDs, savings bonds, brokerage accounts, IRAs, 401K, and 403B accounts.

INSTITUTION	ACCOUNT TYPE & NUMBER	PAPERWORK LOCATION	CONTACT INFORMATION	USERNAME & PASSWORD

INSTITUTION	ACCOUNT TYPE & NUMBER	PAPERWORK LOCATION	CONTACT INFORMATION	USERNAME AND PASSWORD

NON-FINANCIAL ASSETS (houses, boats, etc.)

Here you will note only major assets (cars, houses, boats, jewelry, guns, paintings, collectibles, etc.) If keys and or title insurance is needed to use items, list the location of those, also. You do not want to leave valuables in a house if you are going to be away for a long time. Selling these if you no longer want them could be a good source of funds if you need the money.

PROPERTY	CURRENT VALUE	AMOUNT OWED	ASSET ALLOCATION	ADDITIONAL INFORMTION

LIABILITIES

Include loans, mortgages, notes, and charge cards.

COMPANY	PURPOSE OF LOAN	AMOUNT OWED	PAYMENT TERMS
TOTAL UNPAID BALANCES			

MEMBERSHIPS AND SERVICES

List all the current subscriptions and organizations where you are paying dues, including gym memberships.

ORGANIZATION	SUBSCRIPTION FREQUENCY	PAYMENT FREQUENCY	CONTACT INFORMATION

EMAIL PROVIDERS, SOCIAL MEDIA, AND ONLINE ACCOUNTS

List the passwords and online access information for key accounts. Note if any are paid accounts.

ACCOUNT NAME	USERNAME	PASSWORD	REASON FOR ACCOUNT

ACCOUNT NAME	USER NAME	PASSWORDS	REASON FOR ACCOUNT

VOLUNTEER ACTIVITIES

List the contact information for all groups where you currently volunteer. Identify what activities you are involved in for each organization.

ORGANICATION	CONTACT NAME	CONTACT INFORMATION	ACTIVITIES

OTHER USEFUL PERSONAL INFORMATION

Include any information that you might want someone who is helping you to know, perhaps information about your pets (groomer, vet, kennel, meds, insurance), your church, providers of home repair services, housekeeper, who has the keys to your house, charities you support, and car maintenance records. Include the location of warranty deeds and product guides for household appliances.

OTHER USEFUL INFORMATION	LOCATION

OTHER USEFUL INFORMATION	LOCATION

KEY MEDICAL INFORMATION

This is a good place to note anything you want others to know about your medical information, including whatever brand of medicine it is that you take. For example, I tend to have a strong sensitivity to medicines and often can get by with a pediatric dose of pain meds.

Do not assume that your medical information will be correct in ANY electronic medical system. Not every doctor's office has your medical records uploaded to the system. Nor will all of it be entered correctly and sometimes it can't be retrieved. So it is good to have your own information readily available for others. Seeing that information in documents that you have written will give added credibility to what your electronic records will show. You want your advocate to have the most accurate information possible to help you.

KEY MEDICAL AND DENTAL CONTACT INFORMATION

Include all the medical doctors that you regularly visit and their contact information. Indicate in the first column the type of doctor (GP, dentist, etc.)

DOCTOR'S NAME	PRACTICE TYPE	PHONE	ADDRESS

MEDICINES I TAKE

If you take the brand name versus the generic, make sure to note that on the list. Note any versions of it that you have tried that produced an adverse reaction. Make sure that you note where you keep your medicines. Include who has prescribed the medicines and when you take them. **List the pharmacy where you usually obtain your medicines.** If you are taking allergy shots, note that here, including why you are getting allergy shots and who is giving them to you.

MEDICINES I TAKE	DOSE	FREQUENCY AND TIME OF DAY	PRESCRIBER

ALLERGIES

Note any allergies that you may have to either medicines or non-medicines.

MEDICINES	REACTION

NON-MEDICINES	REACTION

PREVIOUS MAJOR SURGERIES AND PROCEDURES

If you don't know the exact date for some of your past surgeries or who the surgeon was, put your best estimate for the date and the hospital where the surgery was performed. This can be useful information when images are taken to rule out internal scar tissue.

SURGERY NAME	WHAT PURPOSE	SURGEON	DATE PERFORMED

VACCINATIONS

List the last date of each type of vaccine that you have had.

TYPE OF VACCINE	DATE ADMINISTERED	COMMENTS

MAJOR ILLNESSES

Note what illnesses you have had and when you had them, including the start and end dates, if appropriate. You can also note any family medical history for major illnesses.

ILLNESS	DATE	COMMENTS

LABWORK

List most current medical lab work results. Make sure to include the units of measure for the test results.

LATEST LABWORK INFORMATION	RESULTS	DATE

FINAL WISHES

Include the location of organ donor directives, prepaid funeral expenses, final letters, obit, and cremation/burial decision, if you have them.

ITEM	NOTES
Organ Donor Directives	
Prepaid Funeral Expenses	
Letters	
Written instructions for funeral arrangements	
Burial plot deed	
Columbarium niche	
Memorial Service - **Funeral Observances** - **Pallbearers** - **Eulogies** - **Music**	
Disposition of ashes/body	
Obituary	
Charities for donations